TULIPS, WATER, ASH

For Faith,
Welly, writer and
fellow-traveler —

7/20 10

TULIPS,

WATER,

ASH

Lisa Gluskin Stonestreet

THE 2009 MORSE POETRY PRIZE

Selected & Introduced by Jean Valentine

NORTHEASTERN UNIVERSITY PRESS
Boston
Published by
UNIVERSITY PRESS OF NEW ENGLAND
Hanover and London

NORTHEASTERN UNIVERSITY PRESS
Published by
University Press of New England
One Court Street, Lebanon NH 03766
www.upne.com
© 2009 by Lisa Gluskin Stonestreet
Printed in the United States of America
5 4 3 2 1

University Press of New England is a
member of the Green Press Initiative. The
paper used in this book meets their minimum
requirement for recycled paper.

Library of Congress
Cataloging-in-Publication Data
Stonestreet, Lisa Gluskin.
Tulips, water, ash / Lisa Gluskin Stonestreet;
selected and introduced by Jean Valentine.
   p. cm. — (The 2009 Morse Poetry Prize)
ISBN 978-1-55553-708-1 (pbk.)
I. Valentine, Jean. II. Title.
PS3619.T687T85   2009
811'.6 — dc22   2009024771

for E. S.

We do not invent our consciousness.
Here attending is the equal of discovery,
since by the time we can conceive of
a change, the grounds for it are already
in us.

ROBERT IRWIN

CONTENTS

III

Many thanks to the San Francisco Foundation, Universities West Press, the Millay Colony for the Arts, the Vermont Studio Center, the Warren Wilson MFA Program for Writers, and the Jacob K. Javits Fellowships Program, whose generous gifts of money and time helped me to complete this volume, and to believe it worth completing.

Thank you also to the teachers who listened and praised and pushed when I most needed it: Morgan Hewitt Papas, Bob Hanlon, Marcella Torretti, Kim Addonizio, Pimone Triplett, Martha Rhodes, Reg Gibbons, and Marianne Boruch. To friends and fellow makers Yvonne Cannon, Victoria Chang, Cristie Henry, Gina Lain, David Dodd Lee, Louise Mathias, Marie Mutsuki Mockett, Robert Thomas, and everyone in the 13 Ways poetry group. To Jean Valentine, for choosing this collection, and to Guy Rotella, for an editorial eye of rare precision. And to my family, especially and every day to Erich and Truman.

Acknowledgments

Many thanks to the journals and anthologies where the following poems appeared, often in slightly different form:

Bellingham Review: "Against Smoothness"

Best New Poets 2005: "Jars"

Best New Poets 2006: "Spring Forward"

Blackbird: "Dark Matter," "More," "Suburban Pastoral,"
  "View from the Headlands"

Caesura: "The Anthropic Principle," "Double Helix,"
  "Shimmer (Migraine)"

Caffeine Destiny: "Roshambo," "Thought Experiment"

Clackamas Literary Review: "Alluvial"

The Cortland Review: "Desire, Chapter 1," "The Secret
  Lives of Objects"

e: The Emily Dickinson Prize 2003: "Certain,
  Impossible, Likely"

failbetter: "Left-Handed Universe: Variations,"
  "Once Upon a Time"

Gumball Poetry: "Blankness," "Potential"

The Iowa Review: "Spelling Test"

Michigan Quarterly Review: "Spring Forward"

Moby Lives: "Desire, Chapter 1"

New Pages: "Thought Experiment"

Prose Toad: "The Anthropic Principle," "Double Helix,"
  "1982"

Quarterly West: "Persephone at 13"

Red Rock Review: "New York: Ten Months, Two Weeks,
  Three Days"

Spork: "From Then," "1982," *"We're used / by sweetness — "*

Thema: "Roshambo"

Third Coast: "Married Sex"

32 Poems: "Catapult," "De Profundis"

West Branch: "Memoir, Abridged for Publication,"
  "Painting the Existent"

First reading *Tulips, Water, Ash* was a joy for me, and an immediate recognition of craft, mind, and spirit. Since I had the privilege of choosing a Morse Poetry Prize winner, I read it over again several times, over the days, and felt the same sureness of (always subjective) choice.

I admire and rejoice in many qualities of Lisa Gluskin Stonestreet's book: her intelligence, her emotional intelligence as well as her intellectual thirst and her learning, will I think strike the reader at once. Her poems are variously strange, masterful, truthful, scary, and have wonderful, unforced descriptive powers and associative reach and depth.

If there is one defining gift here, I think it is the poet's way of feeling and making art out of shifts of consciousness — often joined to her subtle and tender and bold poems about intimate life.

Her epigraph leads us:

We do not invent our consciousness. Here attending is the equal of discovery, since by the time we can conceive of a change, the grounds for it are already in us. — Robert Irwin

And these words guide us from her first poem to her last.

.   .   .

An example of Stonestreet's descriptive powers is "Blankness." Here is an "I." (and an eye) at nineteen:

There was nothing to look at.

I was nineteen. I took a camera, came in
from the hard-baked heat, came out again . . .

Got down low to the ground, pressed flat to the same soft tar
that filled my frame, shot heat so dry it shone
like water, fifty feet down that slick yellow line.
It was August, two PM, 105. 19__ . I was looking—
bleached-bone hot, open as the shutter, liquid as the road.

A masterful instance of shifts of consciousness moving through and over
sexuality is one of the first poems here, "Jars"; here are a few lines:

> . . . lids off

for everything rolling around in there:
    car and computer crashes (minor), your twisted ankle,
        a marriage (ours), trail of ants swirling

down into the cat dish, basil and dandelions
    leaping up in the yard: What did I think
        would happen? . . .

Last, I would like to quote the final two stanzas of "Falling Off the Edge
of the Earth," for a sense of this poet's occasional brilliant oddness:

Remember too the thinness
of the page, how much you long for a tangent
without end. The heft and swing of things.

No margin there, just the twirling,
the doubling out. The scissoring open,
blood flowing in.

— JEAN VALENTINE

TULIPS, WATER, ASH

out of the depths I cry to you, O Lord

— more like out of the middle, the soft
chewy center of *here*: the mailbox,
the toaster, the dentist office: I cry

to you, or to nothing, I whisper
and roll my eyes: *Oh, lord.*
                    O Lord. Forgive us

our dailiness, our lists of lists.
The gearshift work, the newspaper cutouts,
coupons and cashback in the slow lane.

Whiteboard, whiteout. Little yellow
notes everywhere like moths.
                    Oh, lord. Remember

us, here: the soft warm milky middle,
its erasing breath, its easy arms. Here
where we lie, mostly and meanwhile.

|

These last weeks, so many
    things, just so much and all the mason jars
        filling up with light and oddments, lids off

for everything rolling around in there:
    car and computer crashes (minor), your twisted ankle,
        a marriage (ours), trail of ants swirling

down into the cat dish, basil and dandelions
    leaping up in the yard: What did I think
        would happen? We were transformed,

and obstinate. The phone kept ringing. A bruise
    on my thigh from the suitcase, another
        mid-forearm, shape of a thumb

in brown and blue. New sheets
    on the neighbor's line. I paid bills, juggled
        money and packages. Could not stop

smiling, shivering all at once. Yesterday
    someone left a ring of soft blue pebbles
        on the front steps, where the bus pauses

on its way to the beach. I took out the trash,
     took a call from a friend (her mother's throat
          ringed with tumor). Back in bed, shivering,

then the morning, held down and arching
     toward you. Three jars on the dresser:
          tulips, water, ash.

The longer I know it, my husband says, this place,
the worse I know it is — the ruined,

the once. Paradise once (we think), and still
the hills, the bridge: some perfect gleaming headway,

hills falling down into October, brown, browner, sparks
of the papery eucalyptus. How do you even

talk about that? One person's
glimmering pasts, someone else's ruined moment,

five generations, or three, at the intersection
of Esperanza and Home.

We tracked the last ridge, mustard pollen
clinging to our shoes. The night sure

to devolve into real estate gossip, the way
farmland = strip mall, given enough rope.

The moon hung, or was tethered, low in its cradle.
Down below, headlights, sirens. Women

with their silly little dogs. And behind the first hill
our neighborhood, gentrifying/corroding, strung out

along the streetcar, the sweet, skinny Armenian grocery clerk
hauling in the cantaloupes as the lights go on

in the apartment upstairs. How much more
can I tell you, you who have your own

(broken, ultimate) home? *And the surer*, he said, *I am* —
This untenable near-island, eroding at the edges.

No getting away from the world, at least for now: even on the good days
it's wash and backwash, a humus of cigarette butts and paper moss
on the underfoot. Above the horizon line, it's more like t-shirts and missiles —

even the extra-large gets buried with its future intact. And the bad days?
An endless procession of flashlight beams and last words, saying and said
the same. Each discarded bottle an egg dream, a push to the next

and next. Incanted zygote of heat in the flint, light in the twig, words
on your fingers and in your throat. The radio says *ether,* says *other,*
$\qquad\qquad\qquad\qquad\qquad$ and the reservoir
takes on water, again, bobbing and weaving under its concrete lid.

PAINTING THE EXISTENT

is an act of resistance instigating hope
says Berger, and today in a bout
of homesickness, I see
how hard it is: *there* so compelling:
the pines, cool evening, that other shore
and its rightness might as well be
the past, or next month — in fact for all
I know that's all it is, fodder
for postcard or canvas. And *here?*
Old land safe in its skin, beauty
buffed to human scale. The air weighs down
on mulch and moss, and I crave altitude,
evergreen, the snowmelt and yarrow.

I want gold light on granite, dry wind
in August, rain borne out
on summer burn. But now: the present,
this room, this small window. Pressure
falling on the low hills. *I can pay
attention in just a minute,* I say, *just
as soon as I remember —*

after John Berger

There was nothing to look at.

I was nineteen. I took a camera, came in
from the hard-baked heat, came out again
into a landscape American as sprawl: burned-in
furrows, the space between a thing and its opposite.
Flat arc of white sky, and the field, and the road between.

Got down low to the ground, pressed flat to the same soft tar
that filled my frame, shot heat so dry it shone
like water, fifty feet down that slick yellow line.
It was August, two PM, 105. 19__. I was looking—
bleached-bone hot, open as the shutter, liquid as the road.

THOUGHT EXPERIMENT

Dear, darling, now and now again
we look, and often at the past: that time
with the artichokes or just this morning,
a spring hike, the two groundhogs

and your childish (childhood)
thought: *Everybody's getting it on.*
Well, it *was* the seventies. They were,
and then they weren't . . .

Or we make plans. Imagine,
shall we, a world where we could see
the mundane present — me typing this line,
you making coffee —
only from behind, catch something
in its gait, its smell, and so
make a memory. Or we could hope, hop
forward: project the baby, the big quake,

traffic jam and first hard frost. See:
Yesterday you met me at the train. Next year
is a leap year. All our present
spent elsewhere, a mirror held over the shoulder
and a smaller one, fogged, close to the eye.

Things would still get done, somehow.
Don't look so sad. How else
would there be things to remember?
We must have been there, being here.

Enough. The sages say
be present, through fracture
and fade. Come here, stay
with me, in this small room with the long
white curtains. Here, where we say
this one word: Now.

MARRIED SEX

Not annihilation. Not
that lostness
you'd once do anything for,

to be made
nothing again, known only
in residue: chalk dust, char.

Now you are something else:
not *not*. Turn of wrist,
shudder of hip. Mountain lake

you might enter once and keep entering:
down into granite, glacier,
hold of atom and air. Dazzled

and flayed, made clear,
seen through. Flush all the time
with the seeing.

Selfie do it! screams my friend's child.
And makes the picture. A two-year-old

with a camera. Keeps pushing
the button. Seconds later, pictures

of the floor, *Daddy feet!,* a small
blurred hand. *Selfie take. See!*

Each object distinguished now, carved
from the spinning world, from the next

and next. She moves the cat
into position, tells it to *Stay,*

gives her mother the same command.
Turn the camera around:

When did she stop disappearing
the moment she covered her eyes?

1982

In my locker, shadow-books hovered behind the vents.
I pried one open: mirrors and hair gel.

Fourth period, the class solved for x. I studied
a boy's neck, soft down and new scent.

Indian summer. Mown grass, peat dust,
fields cut to scrub and burn. The dust

blew into corners, between pages,
down the main hall and up the one mountain.

It covered everything. It was another thing.

I memorized theorems, I breathed through the vents.
I thought in sentences.

It settled shallow and broad, like water,
or like oil on water before you shake the jar.

than one, or two, or
enough that counting doesn't help:
a million poppies, a million rats.

Even the former is frightening: anything
that suffocates. Once near Chang Mai,
under a waterfall: little silver fish

like teaspoons, at first a few and then
a dozen, then the school, the whirlwind,
the river a whisk of tarnish . . .

And the scale tips to shiver,
displacement of water for flesh, flashing
and slithering —

it softens the skin, makes the membrane
permeable. As if
they could have carried me off, under

the falls and into — what? Some pure
multiplicity. Soil, silt,
that close and constant air.

PERSEPHONE AT 13

She can swim in and through,
tail flicking, down into the earth
of her own flesh, becoming in her descent
a cell, an electron, small thing spinning
in a great void. We're so far from solid, more dark
than anything —

                  Fourth period, the little fish
(dime-a-dozen under the microscope)
pump ruby spheres through cellophane tails:
down here under the lens it's all tunnels,
jostlings in the hall. The long slow ticking
toward summer: mothers in their cloaks,
preparing to mourn.

                  Dime a dozen, those depths, those five
red jewels. *All the girls are doing it.* Dark matter
richer than loam, its loping song — pull of *away,* of *in.*
The sweet seed she'll eat on the way down.

Halfway through September and the rest
already a long falling, forged notes and forecasts.
Filling in the blanks, mailing them off,

waiting for what came next.
Each day passed in its spiral, hours crouched
over paperbacks and steering wheels. Nights

we tried for momentum, some catapult
of desire that could lift us out of one life
and into the next. Raged, sulked,

pulled down beers at parties, fumbled our way
into each other. Plotted escape from something
not so bad, that is, intolerable.

Each of us not-so-secretly a small thing,
tin and string, spinning wildly
across a table, here at the center of the known universe.

The fashion that year: big shirts
full of wind. Shoes, for running. Tight jeans,
little zippers at the ankle, so nothing could slip out.

SUBURBAN PASTORAL

Maybe there could have been
another life that led us here,
where we ended up:

mapless, dehydrated, telling stories
about cruelty to insects, about
setting little fires — tiny gods

with magnifying glasses. We could
have moved into another house,
the one next door

with the rats, or the other side
with the dandelion problem.
French doors instead of sliding glass.

We got the ants, the picture window.
Plan A, berber, gazebo. Afternoons
where every moment slid down

silently into the moment before:
piling up like cigarette butts,
merit badges, a single summer

of sawdust and parch. Maybe another
life like that, one where it wouldn't matter
how many fires, how long we ran the taps.

Under the street-fair awning, little vats
of balm, treatment for what ails us, therapy

for this dry heat, for the locals
in their straw hats and walking shorts,

lemonade and fried dough no palliative
for the fat babies strapped into strollers, sweating

their way across the moonscape
of Genoa, Nevada: mothers dabbing at foreheads,

winding watches — *grapefruit for positive outlook,*
basil for overactive mind, something

for everyone, and don't we all
have ailments, complaints, desires: for example

the kids shuffling past the country band, wanna-be
b-boys in giant Nikes. Sunburned matrons,

buying up the Kettle Korn and hand-painted
door-knockers. So this is my herb,

my balm: taken-for-granted roadside weed,
two dollars a sprig at Safeway. Homely, hardy,

medicinal. This small brown bottle, and under it
a shifting patch of shade.

FROM THEN

I woke to full code five, perfect iambic
in the upswell. That gift, the taste
of which we're lucky enough
to know, if we're lucky enough —

I should have written it down (I must have
written it down), but. When the earth
closed over I had old envelopes, I had
piles of scrawl. Little tearings at the edges.

The first time — like a secret — I was supposed
to be doing something else. What was meant
to be my (fine) mind moved,

                  but crosswise —

a deep beneath days
of classroom, bedroom, lawn. The sound
folding in the rows and then
that one hum,

            low and sliding: it felt
like grief (or what I thought grief
would feel like). The burn
and lurch of it.

And then it was again, or now,
gone (seeing as I hadn't missed it
until). The world came back,
the dirty linoleum. One shoe squeaking

against the other. I had a new sweater,
a lunch break, a test. I had a sister
and a lock on the door.
                              I lived from then

for the next chance, straight shot of now
in the chatter. It opened up;
it held the pearl. I slipped back down
through a hole in the net.

Use me then, take me
humming and buzzing
down into
hallelujah blankness —
bread salt and oil,
hand on my back,
shape fit to a curve,
iris open past purple
to yellow. Pollen stains
on my hands,
my shirt.

       Use me like the bow
uses the hunter: arrow
arm and eye, that one
moment of sweet forgiving
nothing-elseness. That thing
we're made for.

there was a girl who started reading
and couldn't stop. Holed up
   with a stack of books, she laid them out
where the other girls had dolls, heads

   peeking above the covers. She slept
at the bed edge, chin out. Nights
   she ate them left to right, flashlight buzzing
across the selvage. Began to breakfast

   on words, fill empty space
with line on line. Soon no one
   could see in. At meals, she pushed
the peas around on her plate, hid pages

   under her napkin, ate them later
(1) in the bathtub (2) on the schoolbus
   (3) under the big willow in the backyard.
Mostly she stayed in, opaque

   and opaquer, casting shadows
on the kitchen wall. They got longer
   as the sun went down. It wasn't so bad
out there, she thought, just . . . less.

She kept going, leaving nothing
out — cereal boxes, billboards,
     horoscopes. Long Russian novels
full of war and snow.

     All of it became her, dense center
of a private lode: the music
     she would say, the day
she would turn to the world, inside out.

DESIRE, CHAPTER 1

They met you in your body where you couldn't go alone

and you depended on them, once you found
what they could do   their hands
despite the awkwardness   (for a long time

there was awkwardness   but you didn't know, having nothing
to compare it to):   those hands
with the half-moon nails, calluses

from the guitars   the oars   the paintbrushes
what you found they could do   I mean, you could spend hours
just looking at their hands   in lecture hall, on steering wheels

and at parties.   Even though until then
nothing had happened really — there was this idea first
that they belonged on you, in you   (starfish of the real,

the key to your release. Your adult life: this thing you were saving up for,
incandescent —)   unlike (you thought) the other girls, the ones
with their demure sweaters, and maybe the ones too

in the leather pants, all of whom (you thought)
wanted only the smallest, simplest — You wanted everything.
The luminous, the underwater. You thought their hands held the spark.

No wonder, then: their turns away, the squinting and shuffling.
The sea-green glow of your inner eye.

LEFT-HANDED UNIVERSE: VARIATIONS

1

As a child, my mother was ambidextrous. No traumatic stories or anything:
she'd draw with one hand, color with the other. Later this talent waned,
went the way of the crayon.

2

I wanted very much to be left-handed. I could be a changeling, of course;
the concept explained a lot. I practiced my signature, its cramping line.
The fingers of my right hand crossed.

3

What in our world might indicate the handedness of the universe? All
those quarks: left, right, strange. Everything leaning into a spin.

4

A woman I know married her husband because he moved like Cary Grant.
And all us poor stumblers with *L* and *R* scrawled on the toes of our shoes,
just trying to dance.

5

Different drummer, said my piano teacher, and *perhaps it's best . . . .*

6

Fundamental symmetries: (a) For every particle there must be an equivalent anti-particle with opposite charge. (b) Parity: Left-handed universe should be equal to right-handed universe. (c) If particles are interchanged with anti-particles and left-handed is flipped with right-handed, universe should look identical.

7

The wind comes off the ocean, sweeps the city toward the bay. In mid-September, though, the winds reverse; even the street signs lean west. A few weeks each fall, we drift downhill, forget bus passes and directions. End up where we started.

8

Left-handed, right-handed, saddle-shaped, expanding. Extending the wrong hand, one more time.

AGAINST SMOOTHNESS

Telephone curve and jellybean car,
trucks like muscles, like the big boys
in gym class. Even the teapot's lost its edge.
Soon we'll slip down the narrows
dodging nonexistent corners
in our sculpted shoes. No wind
to resist, slither a skater's ess —
turned dowel, morphic and malleable,
candy curves you can lick or carry,
close in on but never catch.

No grit in your eye, no lint in the trap.
Hurtling down the pneumatic tubes
of our days, offices, weekends,
prayers. Maybe we will be like mercury,
maybe your frictionless skin
will glide by: no resistance, no spark.
Articulation fades, everything down
the silver-gray slide. Goes down easy.
So tempting to rub wrong, bite down, cast out.
To thrust a blade edge into the world.

In 1929, Edwin Hubble theorized that the universe was expanding.
In 1998, scientists found evidence that this expansion was speeding up.

It is only the space between stars.

Only matter, falling away from itself:

the dark and missing
side of the universe —

earth, air, fire, water,
quintessence the fifth element

— everything now is farther but gets there
faster: light in the wires, your hand
as it lifts toward your face, more distant

by an atom than the day before. A spilled drink
moves across the table at six feet
per second, but so too does the cloth.

We have direct evidence from the supernovae.

In the backyard, over the wading pool,
the clothesline: crack and warble

of the satellites, their tethers webbed and straining
above our heads.

EMPRESS OF CUPS

It's coming now; I feel it and try
to remain pleased. The cards
flow from the conjurer's hand and he says
you are being born, these are the new cards.

Rap blasts from Rasputin's,
rolls down Telegraph. Now we're in the pocket,
more silence. Behind me
the lines of the hopeful, hands out

for fortunes they've paid good money
to forget. A girl begs her mother
for a piercing, *or at least a tattoo,*
the wail of that last syllable catching

in the wires above our heads. I can't think
of an image I'd want to carry with me
forever, a self I'd want to dredge up
from the past, clutching its willful deck.

I want to go to bed tonight naked, wake up
in a shower of coins — or rose petals,
I can't remember which. I want a baby,
a book, a knock at the door. I want

a backpack and a gift card
from the household gods. While the stars
are busy realigning, I want to steal away
with the Empress of Cups, her likeness
on my shoulder in erasable ink.

THE RHETORICAL TRIANGLE

Over here, I tell them,
is the subject. In this corner,
the audience (crouched, milling

around a point). And here you are,
the author. This is you! The air conditioner
sucks in smoke. *Your voice*

lives here, in the center. The word
floats unanchored, not that I could
nail it down if I wanted to. It stares;

they stare back. On the mountain,
sap rises to flame. The legs of the triangle
buckle and thrum, go obtuse

then acute. My students
take dutiful notes. One girl
covers her notebook in flames.

SHIMMER (MIGRAINE)

At the first turn everything bends   blurs into light —

a spot that takes up space   eats the spaces between
until there is more of it, wavering, than not;
the cloud (for which you have been waiting   since it gathered
there, on the horizon)   the barometric inversion   the pause —

all stretched out in the moment   before the vase falls
the hovering noose slides itself tight
        and the first shoot goes occipital,
        horizontal —

the light expands and you are saturated,
        pulled into every particle: every sound
        is yours, every bit of

        woodsmoke   street tar   perfume

until you are one receptor
        an eye a prism   going down

convex and collecting, all focus
and your time is up

        .   .   .

You focus
        on the spot, pinpoint then walnut then orange
        behind your right eye
                        (

now in three dimensions (nausea   constriction

pain   the simplest
        the purest)

go away   go away   go away

you hold out   gather it up
to one lead-dense point

but this takes everything   and so   let it all down
        give up volition for the flooding back   the time
        that takes up all space   moves in
        writes the long lease

yes   all right

laying down lines
for the duration

    .   .   .

From the hard sleep   the body's grace:
(sometimes it does not
want to be present; sometimes it accepts the carrot
of oblivion and is grateful)

you move   or breathe   and note first the absence:
searing open *lack*

ratcheted out
until all the ropes loll on the dock

all the corners are sharp, polished
to a shine   all the edges call out to take their place
in the proper world, sidewalk mica
a shower of spark in downtown gray

        and the neon

even in daylight
so green

  absinthe and grass clippings

SPELLING TEST

Outside rained over the tetherballs,
but here I held the world. The joy
of getting it down, down right,
the sharp purple scent of page
under pen — I scratched away
in love with the word.

Number six: squirrel.
Squirrel. It rode the curves,
rolled round the vowel. Again: *squirrel.*
Twisted open in the repetition —
past a small thing quivering. Whiskers,
acorns in a picture book. Pulled into
a turning whorl of sound.

Squirrel. The heady scent of what we call
what we call — by then no more word
than sound, no more sound than itself.

Pure strangeness, and the sweep
of the clock. I handed back my page,
its blank blurred lines. Then the bell,
the door. Tall grass at the edge of the blacktop.

Nothing could be named, though we moved our lips.

A hot day and a woodpecker carves away
at backyard aspen, the dog's ear swiveling
like a tiny satellite dish: pinpoint,
lock on. Morning and the neighborhood
rotates around that point, springing taut
toward equinox. Little flashes call out to those
who can read their language but glitter
for everyone, the planet an ear in a swirl of sound.

In one photograph teletype operators
sit at the alert, collars buttoned high, each finger
rearing back over a single shining key,
each key lit from behind: lone lamppost
spilling glint across filigree and pomade,
skimming even wrought iron with a sheen
of pale sand. Sending it outward,
out here where we keep our images mobile.

That lost hour went somewhere, surely —
out there ready to bank back home
one October midnight, deeper into this
flattened century. Some half-full moon
of the future, and under it a wind-up bird.

THE ANTHROPIC PRINCIPLE

The cosmologist says, *We hope that we don't have to resort to this solution.*

The cheat, the lie, the truth: Orion, for example, is there
because you are there to see it.

But it is one way out.

On the mesa, chill wind:
you take it all in, the light from
the constellation falling, being pulled into
something you can name, trace,
run your finger over the indigo
star chart, its northern reaches flatter and more constant
than that fleeting sky, circumscribed

so you can be there to see it —

Our job as scientists is to identify as many things as possible
that we can explain.

You are there, and how long
you have not been there, how long it has been leading
up to this (mismatched and
unreal though it is, though it
will be still) — Open your view.

Open. Flooding in like stars,
everything, with its hands and its eyes.

All of our parts speak the same language.

Four of a kind is all it takes: a silver-bellied two-step
through heart, finger, hair, hoof and horn.
Vitreous humor, spleen, all thumbs and your hand
spirals down toward completion, stripped-down

telegraph times two carrying the news of the day

and all is catch and fall, rise and carry — a full house
on full alert: synapse flash and the light goes
red, goes crucial, because it's time to do what we do
(that is: breathe, again; use those dog-tired

covalent bonds for something else, but never

something new, that's the beauty of the thing).
Time to stair-step up in the old tongue, speak
the light-revealed tango, your old partner hydrogen
egging you on, oxygen at the right hand, sharp-edged

gimlet carbon, nitrogen, phosphorus the bluestocking aunt,

her long letters on lined paper and you in the corner:
waking, reading, being distinguished from another
and another, the tumblers moving in their locks,
ready to roll, ready for that last-minute substitution:

under the carapace, a line shifts — you, still blindly

nursing your coffee, scratching in those transient
human marks — the suitcases enter the merry-go-round,
the newspapers are retranslated but still the foursome
floats out over the dance floor, quick-steps to a long beat.
Replicant grace, gnawing on its one, old bone.

One up, one down, my favorite option
at the neighborhood taqueria,
and up and down again, a clunk

and a whisper: more perfect perhaps
if it were *shrimp* — pure ring
of oxymoron — but I like it

the way it is, with black beans
and green salsa, giant-minus-one
tortilla fresh from the steam. I like

the almost, the sideways, series built
and then broken: eleven or seven,
the abandoned factory with its grid

of mottled glass, in one corner
the inevitable birdsnest or bullethole.
Or the temptations of hopscotch —

step on a crack, break your mother's back.
I know, I know. How ... expected,
how don't-we-always-want-it-

rough. Some days it's enough,
sitting in the car eating lunch,
watching surfers tempt the waves.

Sun through the windshield,
ice melting in the agua fresca.
And afterwards rolling bits of tinfoil

into tiny silver hearts, lightweight charms
strung out along the dash. Balance
of beans and rice, sting of salsa

where I bit my lip. Helpless,
compelled. I chew it till it bleeds.

Two trains approach Chicago at 50 miles an hour.
Susan has five apples, but James has only two. How much
would you weigh on Jupiter? On Earth? Each pie is divided
into six equal parts. The first train leaves San Francisco
at 6 AM. Remember, an object can't have negative weight.
The New York train will make three stops of an hour each.
If Susan weighs three thousand pounds on Mercury,
will they let her on the train? Did you remember to account
for settling during transport? James, busy converting
Celsius to Fahrenheit, has missed his train entirely. The taxi
charges $2.25 for every half mile or minute in traffic.
The conductor is drunk and we're moving way too fast.

Estimate the likelihood that James and Susan will meet.
Hint: you can slice each pie only once.

MEMOIR, ABRIDGED FOR PUBLICATION

You have a story why not share it.
    Online ad encouraging would-be memoirists

Things happened,
some aspects of which I admit

might have been my fault, though as usual
the opinions of others intervened.

Somewhere around midnight,
events got out of control.

I can say that now.

That's often the way
it went. Mornings, though,

motes shimmered in the east
window; oh, yes, there were

windows. And meals, full
of butter and sexual tension.

At one point the police showed up.

There was the question
of the swimming pool, its ripples

and undulations. Underwater light
on nobody's thighs.

Things changed after that.
People started making comments.

The neighborhood dogs,
quite possibly, knew too much.

Have I mentioned the police?
In the end I found

it best to leave, to take
the train and the money

no matter the how. Looking back,
I must have left

evidence, the why and wherefore: even after
everything, I must

have been the who.

THE FUTURE OF THE PAST

Someone told me: Your cells
replace themselves every seven years. I spent
hours in front of the mirror, time waiting

for time to stop, for the odometer
to click over. I was six: *any minute now
I won't be what I was when I started.*

And another seven, aeons distant?
If *I* were gone then I was — what?
The bruise, the chipped tooth, the stupid

thing I said in school . . . .
Still there. My image fogged
with waiting. I bit my nails, picked at a spot

on my chin. Plotted escape,
told stories, walked around in my body
again and again until it began

to fit, to become itself, even as the mist
built up: calluses at fingers and heels,
dull shine of an ancient scar.

And at thirty-five, five times replaced?
Standing and squinting. Wiping it away
with the edge of my sleeve.

There's a comfort to it, the idea
of an edge, against which —

A point on a plane. Instead of this:
head thrown back, knees bent, hanging on
to this hurtling rock —

Against which one may position oneself.
But it's no use in the abstract; remember

the compass in its velvet box.
Remember proofs: thus and therefore.
The soft purple nap of it, the lean and pull

of those tidal arcs. Swinging it open,
parsing it down. Finding some edge,
some *a* solid and irreducible in its prime.

Remember too the thinness
of the page, how much you long for a tangent
without end. The heft and swing of things.

No margin there, just the twirling,
the doubling out. The scissoring open,
blood flowing in.

THE SECRET LIVES OF OBJECTS

My friend, the engineer, sees hurt machines
— a car grinding its gears, a discarded vise —
and aches. He knows what they know.

The rusted fan, the flea-market eggbeater
share all innocent objects' silence. They speak,
are heard, only through us; need us

like we need the gods, the animating breath
of their care and caprice. The burnishing
or breaking of their use. Objects, my friend says,

they long for patina, and I think of my shelf at home,
the levels and files, my grandfather's folding ruler
and the plumb bob in the window, swaying

beside the jamb. We look and say *file* or *flashlight,*
wooden spoon or *cpu*. We explain them,
and they look to us, mute, fallible —

as if they were looking for something simple.
As if what they were looking for
never tarnished, never fell.

NEW YORK: TEN MONTHS, TWO WEEKS, THREE DAYS

Day one I saw what I couldn't yet say —
how the wet, heavy noise forces out
the rest, how the soot
works its way in.

Cell to cell, day to day to day,
each hive joined with the next until I was one
buzzing, damped by Benadryl,
monthly flaring like a siren.

Stunned slow by multiplicity,
a part out of place in the wrong machine,
I wedged. Interior, migrainous.
Refusing to budge.

Until the city erupted in me,
sent me home beyond won or lost:
stripped down, silent, harder despite myself.

A CONSTANCY

Let me offer you this, one slow
outpouring. Except
I falter. The lines are blocked,
the car won't start and I'm flooded
with guilt, the small clamorings.
Darling, I am inconstant. The roads
fill with snow, then clear,
then snow again and in the summers
with dust. Sometimes
the trucks get through. Meanwhile I want
and want. You face fierce armies,
they rage over the dead.
I would slay them all in your name.
But their deaths are —
deaths. I can give to you
only this day, sky burned white,
my stance at the center of the plain.

It will end, all
of it. It will end. Beyond you
is finite, down only to the last,

they say, who remembers
your face, or (generous now)
your name. Your words

deflect the flesh, but rock
in time covers paper,
not the other way round.

Scissors, though, are true,
if only to confetti — which flares
again as newsprint and Duraflame,

the blades meanwhile
lost to stone (that one
we got right). Rock will end

only in fire, our secret
weapon — allowed once only ever,
I mean ever.

Make paper, the most fragile.
Consign it to fire. Do it again
and again —

matchless, burning, gone.

Gears and levers, a bucket
at the end of a rope. Oak or ash,
soaked soft wood of the bucket,

all the buckets, dug out
by their contents, *made*
of their burdens. And rust:

rust flaking down into it, down
where the pulleys creak their way
through the ancient choreography,

where they reach the river,
its reds and browns. They stay there
for a while, passing their secrets

back and forth in the shallow light —
a rusted swingset and the pull of metal
forward, then back. Dotted swiss.

The buckets come up in a tangle,
or alone, through ropes and beams
and levers, the enormous weave:

Sun bleaching the courtyard, dry weeds
on a stucco wall. Heat in waves.
The fat black sheen of spider,

her dull red spot. Swings creak
on their chains, carrying something slow
up from underneath.

Silver, silver my city burnished far
beyond what I can bear, the branches,
the stripping-down, the year's
hint of new wood. We've worn a path
down the floorboards, twin trails. *It's not used up*
it's just resting. And still the shell
is breaking, albumen gone white
to silver, ghosted inside its orb. Leave its luster
on the side of the hills. Leave its deaths
and its marriages, orange trucks
bearing away what is tarnished, lost lamps
worn to glint and cord. When we leave
for the mountains, you promise, you will bring
the abalone shell, the one that needs
just a little light.

LIGHT AS THE ONLY CONSTANT IN THE UNIVERSE

What is illuminated is what
is reflective, even
a little bit — roughed-up
enough to grab onto, send

something back. Even velvet,
even deep water, pale fish,
candescent eyes
source of their own flare.

Even up here:
dandelion–asphalt–ticketstub.
Axon and dendrite. Mars
in August, in the east.

Little objects with hooks
on them, waiting
for something to catch.
Fragments and shards, fodder

for the seeing.

in last night's dream, the perfect
pair of shoes: they massaged her feet
and went with everything, but the price

kept changing. She lost herself in the alleys
by the souvenir market, some tropical
destination, whitewash and polo shirts.

Spotted a friend, vast corona
of ringlets carried aloft through the streets
just paces ahead: on her way to the hospital,

or the wedding? (Remember when
nothing seemed solid, or everything
possible, depending on the light?)

Even in sleep, how grateful she is
for the morning's patch of ground. This small
green island at rest for a time,

the world sliding around it
a rush of parentheses,
weather fronts, stars.

ALLUVIAL

relating to, composed of, or found in alluvium (alluvia, soil) (alluvia, diamonds)

The build-up, the accretion and you wonder
why you ever bothered, all the little objects — why not
a perfect silence, a white sheet: cool and opalescent,
tracking the sun. Then yesterday the dream of blue
ice, pure balance. But with it your echoing voice. Plains.

Here, now: the compound, the rough. Something mars
the surface, lets itself in. Crumbs everywhere, toast and time
flaking away. Maybe it will fill you
from the inside, squeeze out with each turn and cough.
Hard to see yourself against the background.

Then was a brilliant nothing, star burned clean
in its oneness. Now your days are multiple, dog hair and dust
in three dimensions. Silt on the banks and in the doorways:
making and making. You are grabbed from behind,
held. The water from the tap bathing every dirty dish.

and I'm up there on the mountaintop, my sister says,
and she's telling me about her father —

car abandoned, body never found,

                           the friend and her mother
hung out together on a long line
of not-knowing. Light in an alleyway,

his wallet still on the dash.

                      And now here I'm supposed
to detail something even worse, a whole family
down the street gone, laid out in newsprint and bulletin.

Body in the water, pins on a map.
Looking, and looking away.

                    Or: Another one's twins
lost at twenty-two weeks. I say it too; I'm not
immune, or strong, or maybe cruel enough.

— Like a set of housekeys.

                Have you lost someone?

*[Pp. of **lose**. M.E.* losen, *from O.E.* losian, *to perish.]*

                                                    My infant son
plays a game with his pink rubber ball: he hides it
and when he lifts the pillow, there it is!

Lord save us from the etymologists. Or is it
the talk-show hosts. *Show don't tell,* we say,
but that can't have been what we were talking about.

For example: One of them had a broken back.
For example: *I'm so sorry for your loss.*

The ball is still there. He can do this for hours.

We stood on a streetcorner
clutching our children, noses buried in their pliable scalps.

It is so unfair to end this:
                              They found him. Or
                              They never found him.

And then we went out for kung pao tofu, and home to bed,
and I kissed my son on his head and sang to him,

first the song about the angels and then the one about the sky.

"De Profundis" takes its title from Psalm 129, the first line of which begins the poem.

"Painting the Existent": The poem's first line is quoted from John Berger's essay "Steps Towards a Small Theory of the Visible," in *The Shape of a Pocket* (Pantheon Books, 2001).

"*We're used / by sweetness* — ": The title quotation is taken from Kay Ryan's poem "That Vase of Lilacs."

"Desire, Chapter 1": The first line is quoted from Brenda Hillman's poem "The Spark."

"Left-Handed Universe: Variations": Text in stanza six is quoted from a handout for a course in elementary physics taught by Scott Pratt and Jon Pumplin at Michigan State University.

"Dark Matter": Astronomers infer that some matter, invisible to current modes of detection, exists in the more than 80 percent of space once believed empty. Its presence is linked to ideas about the continuing expansion of the universe. Italicized lines are quoted from the February 25, 2000, airing of the National Public Radio show "Talk of the Nation: Science Friday."

"Empress of Cups": The Empress of Cups (more often Queen of Cups) is a card in the tarot deck, said to represent authentic expression and deepening of emotional consciousness. She is associated with integrity, and also with literal and metaphorical motherhood — giving birth to a child, to self, to honest expression through word or image.

"The Anthropic Principle" explores one attempt by theoretical cosmologists to address the question "why does the universe exist?" The answer: because we are here to perceive it. This makes even theoretical cosmologists nervous.

The form of "Double Helix" replicates, as best I know it, genetic sequencing using the bases adenine (A), thymine (T), cytosine (C), and guanine (G) — the building blocks of human DNA — and the "fifth base" uracil (U) — the variant of thymine that signals the chain of RNA to stop at a given point, and distinguishes the static DNA from the changeable, and changing, RNA. The line "Four of a kind is all it takes" paraphrases a line from "Cosmic Strip," a series of drawings by the artist Matthew Ritchie.

"The Secret Lives of Objects": The phrase "share[s] all innocent objects' silence" is taken from Marilyn Hacker's poem "Scars on Paper."

"Roshambo": Another name for the children's game Rock, Paper, Scissors.

The title of "The Mechanics of Memory" is from a line in Antonio D'Amasio's book *The Feeling of What Happens: Body and Emotion in the Making of Consciousness.*

"Light as the Only Constant in the Universe": The title is taken from Einstein's Special Theory of Relativity.

"For Example" takes the image of the "small green island" from Louise Mathias's poem "Autumn Sequester."

A NOTE ON THE AUTHOR

After working as an arts magazine publisher,
gift wrapper, film studio gofer, and cocktail waitress,
Lisa Gluskin Stonestreet now makes her living as a
freelance editor. She holds an MFA from the Warren
Wilson MFA Program for Writers; her poems have
been awarded a Javits fellowship and Phelan Award,
and have appeared in journals such as *Blackbird*,
The Iowa Review, *Michigan Quarterly Review*, *Third
Coast*, and *32 Poems*, and in the anthologies *Best
New Poets 2005* and *2006*. She lives in San Francisco
with her husband and son.

A NOTE ON THE PRIZE

The Samuel French Morse Poetry Prize was
established in 1983 by the Northeastern University
Department of English in order to honor Professor
Morse's distinguished career as teacher, scholar,
and poet. The members of the prize committee are
Francis C. Blessington, Joseph deRoche, Victor
Howes, David Kellogg, Ellen Noonan, Stuart
Peterfreund, and Guy Rotella.